P9-DGM-879

TEAMWORK

101

WHAT EVERY LEADER NEEDS TO KNOW

JOHN C. MAXWELL

THOMAS NELSON
Since 1798

NASHVILLE DALLAS MEXICO CITY RIO DE JANEIRO BEIJING

© 2008 by John C. Maxwell

All rights reserved. No portion of this book may be reproduced, stored in a retrieval system, or transmitted in any form or by any means—electronic, mechanical, photocopy, recording, scanning, or other—except for brief quotations in critical reviews or articles, without the prior written permission of the publisher.

Published in Nashville, Tennessee, by Thomas Nelson. Thomas Nelson is a registered trademark of Thomas Nelson, Inc.

Published in association with Yates & Yates, www.yates2.com

Thomas Nelson, Inc., titles may be purchased in bulk for educational, business, fund-raising, or sales promotional use. For information, please e-mail SpecialMarkets@ ThomasNelson.com.

Portions of this book have been previously published in *The 17 Indisputable Laws of Teamwork, Talent Is Never Enough, Developing Leaders Around You, The 360° Leader, Winning with People, The 21 Irrefutable Laws of Leadership,* and *The 17 Essential Qualities of a Team Player* by John C. Maxwell.

Library of Congress Cataloging-in-Publication Data

Maxwell, John C., 1947–
    Teamwork 101 : what every leader needs to know / John C. Maxwell.
       p. cm.
    Includes bibliographical references.
    ISBN 978-1-4002-8025-4
    1. Teams in the workplace. 2. Teams in the workplace—Psychological aspects. I. Title. II. Title: Teamwork one hundred one. III. Title: Teamwork one hundred and one.
    HD66.M379 2009
    658.4'022—dc22

                        2009028195

Printed in the United States of America

11 12 13 QG 9 8 7 6 5 4

Contents

PREFACE

I've been passionate about personal growth for most of my life. In fact, I've created and pursued a plan for growth every year for the last forty years! People say that wisdom comes with age. I don't believe that's true. Sometimes age comes alone. I wouldn't have achieved any of my dreams had I not been dedicated to continual improvement. If you want to grow and become the best person you can be, you've got to be intentional about it.

At the same time, life is busy and complex. Most people run out of day long before their to-do lists are done. And trying to get to the bottom line in just about any area of life can be a challenge. Did you know that more new information has been produced in the last thirty years than in the previous five thousand? A single weekday edition of the *New York Times* contains more information than most people in seventeenth-century England were likely to encounter in their lifetimes.

That's why we've developed this series of 101 books. We've cherry-picked the essentials in subjects such as leadership, attitude, relationships, teamwork, and mentoring, and put them into a format that you very likely can read in one sitting. Or you can easily toss a 101 book into a briefcase or purse and read here and there as time allows.

In many of my larger books, I go into my subject in great depth. I do that because I believe it is often the best way to add value to people. *Teamwork 101* is different. It is an introduction to a subject, not the "advanced course." But I believe it will help you on your way to significant growth in this area of your life.

PART I

THE POWER OF TEAMWORK

Why Is Teamwork
So Important?

One is too small a number to achieve greatness.

Who are your personal heroes? Okay, maybe you don't have heroes exactly. Then let me ask you this: Which people do you admire most? Who do you wish you were more like? Which people fire you up and get your juices flowing? Do you admire . . .

- Business innovators, such as Jeff Bezos, Fred Smith, or Bill Gates?
- Great athletes, such as Michael Jordan, Marion Jones, or Mark McGwire?
- Creative geniuses, such as Pablo Picasso, Buckminster Fuller, or Wolfgang Amadeus Mozart?
- Pop-culture icons, such as Madonna, Andy Warhol, or Elvis Presley?

- Spiritual leaders, such as John Wesley, Billy Graham, or Mother Teresa?
- Political leaders, such as Charlemagne, Alexander the Great, or Winston Churchill?
- Revolutionary thinkers, such as Marie Curie, Thomas Edison, or Albert Einstein?

Or maybe your list includes people in a field I did not mention.

It's safe to say that we all admire achievers. And we Americans especially love pioneers and bold individualists, people who fight alone, despite the odds or opposition: the settler who carves a place for himself in the wilds of the frontier, the Old West sheriff who resolutely faces an enemy in a gunfight, the pilot who bravely flies solo across the Atlantic Ocean, and the scientist who changes the world through the power of his mind.

THE MYTH OF THE LONE RANGER

Nothing of significance was ever achieved by an individual acting alone. Look below the surface and you will find that all seemingly solo acts are really team efforts. Frontiersman

Daniel Boone had companions from the Transylvania Company as he blazed the Wilderness Road. Sheriff Wyatt Earp had his two brothers and Doc Holliday looking out for him. Aviator Charles Lindbergh had the backing of nine businessmen from St. Louis and the services of the Ryan Aeronautical Company, which built his plane. Even Albert Einstein, the scientist who revolutionized the world with his theory of relativity, didn't work in a vacuum. Of the debt he owed to others for his work, Einstein once remarked, "Many times a day I realize how much my own outer and inner life is built upon the labors of my fellow men, both living and dead, and how earnestly I must exert myself in order to give in return as much as I have received." It's true that the history of our country is marked by the accomplishments of many strong leaders and innovative individuals who took considerable risks. But those people always were part of teams.

Economist Lester C. Thurow commented:

There is nothing antithetical in American history, culture, or traditions to teamwork. Teams were important in America's history—wagon trains conquered the West, men working together on the assembly line in American industry conquered the world, a successful national strategy and a lot of teamwork put an American on the moon first (and thus far, last). But American mythology extols only the individual . . . In America, halls of fame exist for almost every conceivable activity, but nowhere do Americans raise monuments in praise of teamwork.

I must say that I don't agree with all of Thurow's conclusions. After all, I've seen the U.S. Marine Corps war memorial in Washington, D.C., commemorating the raising of the flag on Iwo Jima. But he is right about something. Teamwork is and always has been essential to building this country. And that statement can be made about every country around the world.

THE VALUE OF TEAMWORK

A Chinese proverb states, "Behind an able man there are always other able men." The truth is that teamwork is at the heart of great achievement. The question isn't whether teams have value. The question is whether we acknowledge that fact and become better team players. That's why I assert that *one is too small a number to achieve greatness.* You cannot do anything of *real* value alone.

I challenge you to think of *one* act of genuine significance in the history of humankind that was performed by a lone human being. No matter what you name, you will find that a team of people was involved. That is why President Lyndon Johnson said, "There are no problems we cannot solve together, and very few that we can solve by ourselves."

C. Gene Wilkes, in his book *Jesus on Leadership*, observed that the power of teams not only is evident in today's modern business world, but it also has a deep history that is evident even in biblical times. Wilkes asserts:

- Teams involve more people, thus affording more resources, ideas, and energy than would an individual.
- Teams maximize a leader's potential and minimize her weaknesses. Strengths and weaknesses are more exposed in individuals.
- Teams provide multiple perspectives on how to meet a need or reach a goal, thus devising several alternatives for each situation. Individual insight is seldom as broad and deep as a group's when it takes on a problem.
- Teams share the credit for victories and the blame for losses. This fosters genuine humility and authentic

community. Individuals take credit and blame alone. This fosters pride and sometimes a sense of failure.
- Teams keep leaders accountable for the goal. Individuals connected to no one can change the goal without accountability.
- Teams can simply do more than an individual.

If you want to reach your potential or strive for the seemingly impossible—such as communicating your message two thousand years after you are gone—you need to become a team player. It may be a cliché, but it is nonetheless true: Individuals play the game, but teams win championships.

WHY DO WE STAND ALONE?

Knowing all that we do about the potential of teams, why do some people still want to do things by themselves? I believe there are a number of reasons.

1. EGO

Few people are fond of admitting that they can't do everything, yet that is a reality of life. There are no supermen or superwomen. As Kerry Walls, one of the people on my INJOY Group team, says, "Spinning more plates doesn't increase your talent—it increases your likelihood of dropping a plate." So the question is not whether you can do everything by yourself; it's how soon you're going to realize that you can't.

Philanthropist Andrew Carnegie declared, "It marks a big step in your development when you come to realize that other people can help you do a better job than you could do alone." To do something really big, let go of your ego, and get ready to be part of a team.

2. INSECURITY

In my work with leaders, I've found that some individuals fail to promote teamwork because they feel threatened by other people. Sixteenth-century Florentine statesman Niccolo Machiavelli probably made similar observations, prompting him to write, "The first method for estimating the intelligence of a ruler is to look at the men he has around him."

I believe that insecurity, rather than poor judgment or lack of intelligence, most often causes leaders to surround themselves with weak people. As I stated in *The 21 Irrefutable Laws of Leadership*, only secure leaders give power to others.

That is the Law of Empowerment. On the other hand, insecure leaders usually fail to build teams because of one of two reasons: either they want to maintain control over everything for which they are responsible, or they fear being replaced by someone more capable. In either case, leaders who fail to promote teamwork undermine their own potential and erode the best efforts of the people with whom they work. They would benefit from the advice of President Woodrow Wilson: "We should not only use all the brains we have, but all that we can borrow."

3. NAÏVETÉ

Consultant John Ghegan keeps a sign on his desk that says, "If I had it to do all over again, I'd get help." That remark accurately represents the feelings of the third type of people who fail to become team builders. They naively underestimate the difficulty of achieving big things. As a result, they try to go it alone.

Some people who start out in this group turn out okay in the end. They discover that their dreams are bigger than their capabilities, they realize they won't accomplish their goals solo, and they adjust. They make team building their approach to achievement. But some others learn the truth too late, and as a result, they never accomplish their goals. And that's a shame.

4. Temperament

Some people aren't very outgoing and simply don't think in terms of team building and team participation. As they face challenges, it never occurs to them to enlist others to achieve something.

As a people person, I find that hard to relate to. Whenever I face any kind of challenge, the very first thing I do is think about the people I want on the team to help with it. I've been that way since I was a kid. I've always thought, *Why take the journey alone when you can invite others along with you?*

I understand that not everyone operates that way. But whether or not you are naturally inclined to be part of a team is really irrelevant. If you do everything alone and never partner with other people, you create huge barriers to your own potential. Dr. Allan Fromme quipped, "People have been known to achieve more as a result of working with others than against them." What an understatement! It takes a team to do anything of lasting value. Besides, even the most introverted person in the world can learn to enjoy the benefits of being on a team. (That's true even if someone isn't trying to accomplish something great.)

My friend Chuck Swindoll wrote a piece in *The Finishing Touch* that sums up the importance of teamwork:

Nobody is a whole team . . . We need each other. You need someone and someone needs you. Isolated islands we're not. To make this thing called life work, we gotta lean and support. And relate and respond. And give and take. And confess and forgive. And reach out and embrace and rely . . . Since none of us is a whole, independent, self-sufficient, super-capable, all-powerful hotshot, let's quit acting like we are. Life's lonely enough without our playing that silly role. The game is over. Let's link up.

For the person trying to do everything alone, the game really is over. If you want to do something big, you must link up with others. One is too small a number to achieve greatness.

2

WHAT IS THE IMPACT OF
GOOD TEAMWORK?

There are some things only a team can accomplish.

I recently had the opportunity to tour the aircraft carrier USS *Enterprise* while it was at sea. The entire experience was fantastic, but the highlight for me was sitting with Rear Admiral Raymond Spicer, commander of the *Enterprise*'s carrier strike group, and watching F/A-18 Hornet jets taking off and landing at night. What an incredible sight!

There was beauty in the way the jets shot off the deck and others landed, coming to a halt in a mere two seconds. But what struck me even more was the number of people who seemed to be involved in the process and the teamwork that was required. When I asked Admiral Spicer about it, he put me in contact with Lt. Commander Ryan Smith, the V2 Division officer, who explained the process to me. He said:

The pilot is seated at the controls of an F/A-18 Hornet as the jet is accelerated from 0 to nearly 160 mph in the span of less than three seconds. As the aircraft climbs away from the carrier, she raises the landing gear and is suddenly alone in the black of night. There are few examples of solitary combat in today's era of modern, networked warfare, but an aviator seated in the cockpit of one of today's Navy fighters still seems like an example in which the accomplishment of a particular objective is entirely dependent on the talent, skill, and effort of one particular, highly trained individual. However, the singular act of catapulting a jet off of the end of one of these carriers is the result of the complex orchestration of scores of individuals, each with a mastery of his or her own specific task. It is the efforts and coordination of these individuals, most of whom are just barely high school graduates, which serve as a truly inspiring example of teamwork.[1]

He then went on to explain the process. Hours before that jet taxis to the catapult for launching, it is being inspected by a team of mechanics and technicians. While the pilot is receiving a briefing on the mission, including weather, target information, radio procedures, and navigational information (all of which are produced by teams of sailors), the aircraft is going through an equally rigorous period of preparation. The preflight routine ends only when the pilot has reviewed the aircraft's maintenance records and inspected the aircraft for flight.

Thirty minutes prior to the aircraft's launch time, a specific sequence of steps begins that is always followed with precision. The aircraft carrier's air boss calls for engine starts, a test to make certain that the jets are in proper working order, while the pilot runs through his pre-taxi checks. The aircraft's plane captain is listening to the engines and watching the movement of each control surface as the pilot does his checks. Once it is determined that everything is okay, the aircraft is then topped off with fuel.

Meanwhile, the aircraft handling officer, seated in flight deck control and using a tabletop model of the carrier's flight deck and aircraft, reviews the launch sequence plan with the deck caller. The aircraft handling officer radios the deck caller, telling him which aircraft are reported to be "up" and ready to taxi.

The deck caller leads three separate teams of plane directors and other sailors from the carrier's Flight Deck Division, and each team is responsible for a different area of the flight deck. These teams ensure that each aircraft to be launched is safely unchained, directed around other parked aircraft (often with only inches of clearance), and put in line to be launched—sometimes as the deck of the carrier is pitching and rolling. When the deck caller gets the okay, the aircraft goes to one of the four catapults.

On deck, final maintenance checkers walk alongside the aircraft and inspect each panel and component as crew members from the Catapult and Arresting Gear Division hook the aircraft up to the catapult mechanism and ready it for launch. Below deck, other teams are using hydraulics and other equipment to control steam from the nuclear reactor that will be used to power the catapult.

At this time, ordnance personnel arm the aircraft's weapons. The catapult officer then confirms the weight of the aircraft with the pilot. He also makes note of the wind over the deck and ambient conditions. He performs calculations to determine the precise amount of energy needed to achieve flight.

Even with all of this preparation, no jet would be able to take off if the ship weren't in the proper position. The ship's navigational team, which makes calculations to determine the required speed and heading, has relayed information to the bridge, and by now the ship has completed its turn and has accelerated to proper speed on its directed course. The aircraft is finally almost ready for launch.

The aircraft is hydraulically tensioned into the catapult. At this point, the pilot applies full power to the aircraft's engines and checks to be sure the aircraft is functioning. If the pilot determines that the aircraft is ready for flight, he signals the catapult officer by saluting him. If the catapult officer also receives a thumbs-up from the squadron final checker, he will then give the fire signal to a catapult operator who depresses the fire button and sends the aircraft on its way.

What's amazing is that three more aircraft can be launched right behind it in less than a minute, each having gone through that same procedure. And in just a matter of minutes, that same flight deck can be prepared to receive landing aircraft, one coming on final approach just as the previous one is taxied out of the landing area.

Teamwork Truths

I can think of few things that require such a high degree of precision teamwork with so many different groups of people as the launching of a jet from an aircraft carrier. It's easy to see that teamwork is essential for the task. However, a task doesn't *have* to be complex to need teamwork. In 2001, when I wrote *The 17 Indisputable Laws of Teamwork*, the first law I included was the Law of Significance, which says, "One is too small a number to achieve greatness." If you want to do anything of value, teamwork is required.

Teamwork not only allows a person to do what he couldn't otherwise do; it also has a compounding effect on all he possesses—including talent. If you believe one person is a work of God (which I do), then a group of talented people committed to working together is a work of art. Whatever your vision or desire, teamwork makes the dream work.

Working together with other people toward a common goal is one of the most rewarding experiences of life. I've led or been part of many different kinds of teams—sports teams, work teams, business teams, ministry teams, communication teams, choirs, bands, committees, boards, you name it. I've observed teams of nearly every type in my travels around the world. And talking to leaders, developing teams, counseling with coaches, and teaching and writing on teamwork have influenced my thinking when it comes to teams. What I've learned, I want to share with you:

1. Teamwork Divides the Effort and Multiplies the Effect

Would you like to get better results from less work? I think everyone would. That's what teamwork provides.

It's common sense that people working together can do more than an individual working alone. So why are some people reluctant to engage in teamwork? It can be difficult in the beginning. Teams don't usually come together and develop on their own. They require leadership and cooperation. While that may be more work on the front end, the dividends it pays on the back end are tremendous and well worth the effort.

2. Talent Wins Games, but Teamwork Wins Championships

A sign in the New England Patriots' locker room states, "Individuals play the game, but teams win championships." Obviously the Patriot players understand this. Over a four-year period, they won the Super Bowl three times.

Teams that repeatedly win championships are models of teamwork. For more than two decades, the Boston Celtics dominated the NBA. Their team has won more championships than any other in NBA history, and at one point

during the fifties and sixties, the Celtics won eight championships in a row. During their run, the Celtics never had
a player lead the league in scoring. Red Auerbach, who
coached the Celtics and then later moved to their front
office, always emphasized teamwork. He asserted, "One
person seeking glory doesn't accomplish much; everything
we've done has been the result of people working together to
meet our common goals."

It's easy to see the fruit of teamwork in sports. But it is
at least as important in business. Harold S. Geneen, who
was director, president, and CEO of ITT for twenty years,
observed, "The essence of leadership is the ability to inspire
others to work together as a team—to stretch for a common
objective." If you want to perform at the highest possible
level, you need to be part of a team.

3. TEAMWORK IS NOT ABOUT YOU

The Harvard Business School recognizes a team as a
small number of people with complementary skills who are
committed to a common purpose, performance goals, and
approach for which they hold themselves mutually accountable. Getting those people to work together is sometimes a
challenge. It requires good leadership. And the more tal-

ented the team members, the better the leadership that is needed. The true measure of team leadership is not getting people to work. Neither is it getting people to work hard. The true measure of a leader is getting people to work hard together!

I've studied exceptional team leaders and coaches. Here are what just a few say about getting people to work together:

PAUL "BEAR" BRYANT, legendary Alabama football coach: "In order to have a winner, the team must have a feeling of unity. Every player must put the team first ahead of personal glory."

BUD WILKINSON, author of *The Book of Football Wisdom:* "If a team is to reach its potential, each player must be willing to subordinate his personal goals to the good of the team."

LOU HOLTZ, coach of college football national championship teams: "The freedom to do your own thing ends when you have obligations and responsibilities. If you want to fail yourself—you can—but you cannot do your own thing if you have responsibilities to team members."

MICHAEL JORDAN, most talented basketball player of all time and six-time world champion: "There are plenty of teams in every sport that have great players and never win titles. Most of the time, those players aren't willing to sacrifice for the greater good of the team. The funny thing is, in the end, their unwillingness to sacrifice only makes individual goals more difficult to achieve. One thing I believe to the fullest is that if you think and achieve as a team, the individual accolades will take care of themselves. Talent wins games, but teamwork and intelligence win championships."[2]

All great teams are the result of their players making decisions based on what's best for the rest. That's true in sports, business, the military, and volunteer organizations. And it's true at every level, from the part-time support person to the coach or CEO. The best leaders also put their team first. C. Gene Wilkes observed:

Team leaders genuinely believe that they do not have all the answers—so they do not insist on providing them. They believe they do *not* need to make all key decisions—so they do not do so. They believe they *cannot* succeed without the combined contributions of all the other members of the team to a common end—so they avoid any action that might constrain inputs or intimidate anyone on the team. Ego is *not* their predominant concern.

Highly talented teams possess players with strong egos. One secret of successful teamwork is converting individual ego into team confidence, individual sacrifice, and synergy. Pat Riley, NBA champion coach, says, "Teamwork requires that everyone's efforts flow in a single direction. Feelings of significance happen when a team's energy takes on a life of its own."

4. GREAT TEAMS CREATE COMMUNITY

All effective teams create an environment where relationships grow and teammates become connected to one another. To use a term that is currently popular, they create a *sense of community*. That environment of community is based on trust. Little can be accomplished without it.

On good teams, trust is a nonnegotiable. On winning teams, players extend trust to one another. Initially that is a risk because their trust can be violated and they can be hurt.

At the same time that they are giving trust freely, they conduct themselves in such a way to earn trust from others. They hold themselves to a high standard. When everyone gives freely and bonds of trust develop and are tested over time, players begin to have faith in one another. They believe that the person next to them will act with consistency, keep commitments, maintain confidences, and support others. The stronger the sense of community becomes, the greater their potential to work together.

Developing a sense of community in a team does not mean there is never conflict. All teams experience disagreements. All relationships have tension. But you can work them out. My friend Bill Hybels, who leads a congregation of more than twenty thousand people, acknowledges this:

> The popular concept of unity is a fantasy land where disagreements never surface and contrary opinions are never stated with force. Instead of unity, we use the word *community*. We say, "Let's not pretend we never disagree. We're dealing with the lives of 16,000 people [at the time]. The stakes are high. Let's not have people hiding their concerns to protect a false notion of unity. Let's face the disagreement and deal with it in a good way."

> The mark of community . . . is not the absence of conflict. It's the presence of a reconciling spirit. I can have a rough-and-tumble leadership meeting with someone, but because we're committed to the community, we can still leave, slapping each other on the back, saying, "I'm glad we're still on the same team." We know no one's bailing out just because of a conflicting position.

When a team shares a strong sense of community, team members can resolve conflicts without dissolving relationships.

5. Adding Value to Others Adds Value to You

"My husband and I have a very happy marriage," a woman bragged. "There's nothing I wouldn't do for him, and there's nothing he wouldn't do for me. And that's the way we go through life—doing nothing for each other!" That kind of attitude is a certain road to disaster for any team—including a married couple.

Too often people join a team for their personal benefit. They want a supporting cast so that they can be the star. But that attitude hurts the team. When even the most talented person has a mind to serve, special things can happen. Former NBA great Magic Johnson paraphrased John F.

Kennedy when he stated, "Ask not what your teammates can do for you. Ask what you can do for your teammates." That wasn't just talk for Johnson. Over the course of his career with the Los Angeles Lakers, he started in every position during championship games to help his team.

U.S. president Woodrow Wilson asserted, "You are not here merely to make a living. You are here in order to enable the world to live more amply, with greater vision, with a finer spirit of hope and achievement. You are here to enrich the world, and to impoverish yourself if you forget the errand." People who take advantage of others inevitably fail in business and relationships. If you desire to succeed, then live by these four simple words: *add value to others*. That philosophy will take you far.

3

CAN MY TEAM
ACCOMPLISH THE DREAM?

As the challenge escalates, the need for teamwork elevates.

In 1935, twenty-one-year-old Tenzing Norgay made his first trip to Mount Everest. He worked as a porter for a British team of mountaineers. A Sherpa born in the high altitudes of Nepal, Tenzing had been drawn to the mountain from the time that Westerners began visiting the area with the idea of climbing to the mountain's peak. The first group had come in 1920. Fifteen years later, climbers were still trying to figure out how to conquer the mountain.

The farthest this expedition would go was up to the North Col, which was at an altitude of 22,000 feet. (A *col* is a flat area along a mountain's ridge between peaks.) And it was just below that col that the climbing party made a gruesome discovery. They came across a wind-shredded tent. And in that tent was a skeleton with a little frozen skin stretched over the bones. It was sitting in an odd position, with one boot off and the laces of the other boot between its bony fingers.

Harshest Place on the Planet

Mountain climbing is not for the faint of heart, because the world's highest peaks are some of the most inhospitable places on earth. Of course, that hasn't stopped people from attempting to conquer mountains. Everest, the world's highest peak at 29,035 feet, is remote. The altitude incapacitates all but the hardiest and most experienced climbers, and the weather is ruthlessly unforgiving. Experts believe that the bodies of 120 failed climbers remain on the mountain today.[1]

The body Tenzing and the others found in 1935 was that of Maurice Wilson, an Englishman who had sneaked into Tibet and tried to climb the mountain secretly, without the permission of the Tibetan government. Because he was trying to make the ascent quietly, he had hired only three porters to climb the mountain with him. As they approached the North Col, those men had refused to go any farther with him. Wilson decided to try to make the climb on his own. That decision killed him.

MEASURE THE COST

Only someone who has climbed a formidable mountain knows what it takes to make it to the top. For thirty-two years, between 1920 and 1952, seven major expeditions tried—and failed—to make it to the top of Everest. An experienced climber, Tenzing Norgay was on six of those expeditions. His fellow climbers joked that he had a third lung because of his ability to climb tirelessly while carrying heavy loads.

NOT A CASUAL STROLL

In 1953, Tenzing embarked on his seventh expedition to Everest with a British group led by Colonel John Hunt. By then, he was respected not only as a porter who could carry heavy loads at high altitudes, but also as a mountaineer and full-fledged expedition member, an honor unusual at that time for a Sherpa. The year before he had climbed to a height of 28,250 feet with a Swiss team. Up to then, that was the closest any human being had come to the top of the mountain.

Tenzing was also engaged to be the British group's *sirdar* for the trip, the Sherpa leader who would hire, organize, and lead the porters for the journey. That was no small task. To hope to get just two people from base camp up to the summit, the team brought ten high-altitude climbers, including a New Zealander named Edmund Hillary. Altogether, the men would require two and a half *tons* of equipment and food. Those supplies couldn't be trucked or airlifted to the base of the mountain. They had to be delivered to Kathmandu and *carried* on the backs of men and women 180 miles up and down Himalayan ridges and over rivers crossed by narrow rope-and-plank bridges to the base camp. Tenzing would have to hire between two and three hundred people just to get the supplies in the vicinity of the mountain. Supplies needed by the party above the base camp would have to be carried up the mountain by another forty porters, each a Sherpa with extensive mountain experience.

IT TAKES A TEAM

For each level that the climbers reached, a higher degree of teamwork was required. One set of men would exhaust themselves just to get equipment up the mountain for the next group. Two-man teams would work their way up the mountain, finding a path, cutting steps, securing ropes. And then they would be finished, having spent themselves to make the next leg of the climb possible for another team. Of the teamwork involved, Tenzing remarked:

> You do not climb a mountain like Everest by trying to race ahead on your own, or by competing with your comrades. You do it slowly and carefully, by unselfish teamwork. Certainly I wanted to reach the top myself; it was the thing I had dreamed of all my life. But if the lot fell to someone else I would take it like a man, and not a cry-baby. For that is the mountain way.[2]

The team of climbers, using the "mountain way," ultimately made it possible for two pairs to make an attempt at reaching the summit. The first consisted of Tom Bourdillon and Charles Evans. When they tried and failed, the other team got its chance. That team consisted of Tenzing and Edmund Hillary. Tenzing wrote of the first team:

> They were worn-out, sick with exhaustion, and, of course, terribly disappointed that they had not reached the summit themselves. But still . . . they did everything

they could to advise and help us. And I thought, Yes, that is how it is on a mountain. That is how a mountain makes men great. For where would Hillary and I have been without the others? Without the climbers who had made the route and the Sherpas who had carried the loads? It was only because of the work and sacrifice of all of them that we were now to have our chance at the top.[3]

They made the most of their chance. On May 29, 1953, Tenzing Norgay and Edmund Hillary accomplished what no other human being ever had: they stood on the summit of Mount Everest, the world's highest peak!

Could Tenzing and Hillary have made it alone? The answer is no. Could they have made it without a great team? Again, the answer is no. Why? Because *as the challenge escalates, the need for teamwork elevates.* That's the Law of Mount Everest.

WHAT IS YOUR EVEREST?

You may not be a mountain climber, and you may not have any desire to reach the summit of Everest. But I bet you have a dream. I say that with confidence because deep down everybody has one—even the people who haven't figured out what theirs is yet. If you have a dream, you need a team to accomplish it.

How do you approach the task of putting together a team to accomplish your dream? I think the best way to start is to ask yourself three questions:

1. "What Is My Dream?"

It all starts with this question because your answer reveals *what could be*. Robert Greenleaf remarked, "Nothing much happens without a dream. For something really great to happen, it takes a really great dream."

What lies in your heart? What do you see as a possibility for your life? What would you like to accomplish during your time on this earth? Only a dream will tell you such things. As Harlem Renaissance poet Langston Hughes wrote:

> *Hold fast to dreams for if dreams die,*
> *Life is a broken-winged bird that cannot fly.*
> *Hold fast to dreams for when dreams go,*
> *Life is a barren field frozen with snow.*

If you want to do something great, you must have a dream. But a dream is not enough. You can fulfill a dream only if you are part of a team.

2. "WHO IS ON MY TEAM?"

This second question tells you *what is*. It measures your current situation. Your potential is only as good as your current team. That's why you must examine who is joining you on your journey. A mountain climber like Maurice Wilson, who had only three halfhearted companions, was never able to accomplish his dream of climbing the mountain. However, someone like Tenzing Norgay, who always climbed Everest with the best mountaineers in the world, was able to make it to the top. A great dream with a bad team is nothing more than a nightmare.

3. "WHAT SHOULD MY DREAM TEAM LOOK LIKE?"

The truth is that your team must be the size of your dream. If it's not, then you won't achieve it. You simply cannot achieve an ultimate number ten dream with a number four team. It just doesn't happen. If you want to climb Mount Everest, you need a Mount Everest–sized team. There's no other way to do it. It's better to have a great team with a weak dream than a great dream with a weak team.

Focus on the Team, Not the Dream

One mistake I've seen people repeatedly make is focusing too much attention on their dream and too little on their team. But the truth is that if you build the right team, the dream will almost take care of itself.

Every dream brings challenges of its own. The kind of challenge determines the kind of team you need to build. Consider a few examples:

TYPE OF CHALLENGE	TYPE OF TEAM REQUIRED
New challenge	Creative team
Controversial challenge	United team
Changing challenge	Fast and flexible team
Unpleasant challenge	Motivated team
Diversified challenge	Complementary team
Long-term challenge	Determined team
Everest-sized challenge	Experienced team

If you want to achieve your dream—I mean, really do it, not just imagine what it would be like—then grow your team. But as you do so, make sure your motives are right. Some people gather a team just to benefit themselves. Others do it because they enjoy the team experience and want to create a sense of community. Still others do it because they want to build an organization. The funny thing about these reasons is that if you're motivated by *all* of them, then your desire to build a team probably comes from wanting to add value to everyone on the team. But if your desire to build the team comes as the result of only one of these reasons, you probably need to examine your motives.

How to Grow a Team

When the team you have doesn't match up to the team of your dreams, then you have only two choices: Give up your dream, or grow up your team. Here is my recommendation concerning how to do the latter.

1. Develop Team Members

The first step to take with a team that's not realizing its potential is to help individual team members grow. If you're leading the team, then one of your most important responsibilities is to see the potential that people don't see in themselves, and draw it out. When you accomplish this, you're doing your job as a leader.

Think about the people on your team, and determine what they need based on the following categories:

- Enthusiastic beginner—needs direction
- Disillusioned learner—needs coaching
- Cautious completer—needs support
- Self-reliant achiever—needs responsibility

Always give the people who are already on your team a chance to grow and bloom. That's what early British explorer Eric Shipton did with a young, inexperienced kid named Tenzing in 1935, and his country was rewarded eighteen years later with a successful climb of the world's highest peak.

2. Add Key Team Members

Even if you give every person on your team a chance to learn and grow, and all of them make the most of the opportunities, you may find that you still lack the talent needed to accomplish your dream. That's when it's time to recruit that talent. Sometimes all the team needs is one key person with talent in an area to make the difference between success and failure.

3. Change the Leadership

Various team challenges require different kinds of leadership. If a team has the right talent but still isn't growing, sometimes the best thing you can do is ask someone from the team who has previously been a follower to step into a leadership role. That transition may occur only for a short season, or it may be more permanent.

The challenge of the moment often determines the leader for that challenge. Why? Because every person on the team has strengths and weaknesses that come into play. That was the case for the Everest team as they faced every stage of the journey. Colonel Hunt chose the climbers and led the expedition, casting vision, modeling unselfish service, and making critical decisions about who would take which part. Tenzing chose the porters, leading, organizing, and motivating them to build the camps at each stage of the mountain. And the climbing teams took turns leading, cutting the trail up the mountain so that Hillary and Tenzing could make the final climb to the summit. When a particular challenge emerged, so did a leader to meet it. And everyone worked together, doing his part.

If your team is facing a big challenge, and it doesn't seem to be making any progress "up the mountain," then it might be time to change leaders. There may be someone on the team more capable for leading during this season.

4. Remove Ineffective Members

Sometimes a team member can turn a winning team into a losing one, either through lack of skill or a poor attitude. In those cases you must put the team first and make changes for the greater good.

Tenzing faced that situation during the 1953 Everest expedition. During early days of travel, there were continual flare-ups between the porters and the British team of climbers, and as sirdar, Tenzing was constantly stuck in the middle trying to work things out. After repeatedly negotiating the peace between the two parties, Tenzing discovered that the source of the problem was two Sherpas who were stirring up dissension. He promptly fired them and sent them home. Peace was quickly restored. If your team keeps breaking down or falling short, you may need to make changes in your team.

Growing a team is demanding and time-consuming. But if you want to achieve your dream, you have no other choice. The greater the dream, the greater the team. *As the challenge escalates, the need for teamwork elevates.* That is the Law of Mount Everest.

4

HOW DO I DEVELOP
A TEAM THAT LASTS?

Create an environment that unleashes new leaders.

If you are the leader in your organization, then I want to spend a few moments with you in this special section. Many leaders in the middle of organizations are highly frustrated. They have great desire to lead and succeed; yet their leaders are often a greater hindrance than help to them. More than two-thirds of the people who leave their jobs do so because of an ineffective or incompetent leader. People don't leave their company—they leave their leader.

As a leader, you have the power the way nobody else does to create a positive leadership culture where potential leaders flourish. If you create that environment, then people with leadership potential will learn, gain experience, and come into their own. They will become the kind of team leaders who make an organization great.

If you're willing to work at making your organization a place where leaders lead and do it well, you'll need to shift your focus from

> leading the people and the organization, to . . .
> leading the people, finding leaders, and leading the organization, to . . .
> leading the people, developing the leaders, and leading the organization, to . . .
> leading and empowering the leaders while they lead the organization, to . . .
> serving the leaders as they lead the organization.

Depending on where you're starting from, that process may take several years, and it may be a tough climb. But think of the alternative. Where will your organization be in five years if you don't raise up leaders in an environment that unleashes team leaders?

THE LEADER'S DAILY DOZEN

If you're ready to revolutionize your organization, then I want to encourage you to start the process by adopting what

I call the "Leader's Daily Dozen." Every morning when you get up and get ready to lead your organization, make a commitment to these twelve power-unleashing activities.

1. Place a High Value on People

The first shift for turning your organization into a leader-friendly environment must occur inside of you. You only commit yourself to things you value. And fundamentally, if you don't value people, you will never create a culture that develops leaders.

Most leaders focus on two things: the vision and the bottom line. The vision is what usually excites us most, and taking care of the bottom line keeps us in business. But between the vision and the bottom line are all the people in your organization. What's ironic is that if you ignore the people and only pay attention to these other two things, you will lose the people and the vision (and probably the bottom line). But if you focus on the people, you have the potential to win the people, the vision, and the bottom line.

When Jim Collins studied great companies and came to discover and define what he called level five leaders, he noticed that these excellent leaders didn't take the credit for their organization's accomplishments. In fact, they were incredibly humble and gave the credit to their people. Without a doubt, level five leaders place a high value on people.

Many companies say they value their people and their customers. Those are trendy things to say, but talk is cheap. If you want to know whether this is a value in your organization, then talk to people who know your organization well but don't work for it. What would they say? Their answers would probably give you the most accurate picture.

But you know your own heart better than anyone else. It all starts with you. You need to ask yourself: *Do I place a high value on people?*

2. Commit Resources to Develop People

Once when I was flying to Dallas with Zig Ziglar, he asked if I ever received letters from people thanking me. When I acknowledged that I did, he asked, "When you get those letters, what do people thank you for?" I had never really thought about that before, but the answer was clear. People almost always said thanks for a book I had written or some other resource I had produced.

"It's the same for me," Zig said. "Isn't that interesting?

You and I are known for our speaking, but that's not what prompts people to write."

I've done a lot of speaking over the past thirty-five years. I love doing it, and I do think it has value. Events are great for creating lots of energy and enthusiasm, but if you want to facilitate growth, you need resources. They are better for development because they are process oriented. You can take them with you. You can refer back to them. You can dig into the meat and skip the fluff—and you can go at your own pace.

Once when I was teaching leaders at a large corporation, one of the event's organizers stated from the platform that people were their organization's most appreciable asset. I applauded his sentiment, but I also expanded on it for the leaders in the room. His statement is true only if you develop those people.

It takes a lot of effort to develop leaders. The first question a leader usually asks is, "What is it going to cost?" My answer is, "Whatever amount it costs, it won't be as high as the cost of not developing your people."

Once again, I have a question for you. Ask yourself, Am I committed to providing resources for leadership development?

3. Place a High Value on Leadership

People who run a one-person business may not have to worry about leadership. But for people who lead organizations, leadership is always an issue. Anytime you have two or more people working together, leadership comes into play. In some organizations, all the emphasis is placed on effort, and leadership isn't even on people's radar. What a mistake.

All good leaders recognize the importance of leadership and place a high value on it. I love what General Tommy Franks said about the ultimate leaders in the middle of the military—the sergeants:

> The months in the desert had reinforced my longstanding conviction that sergeants really were the backbone of the Army. The average trooper depends on NCOs for leadership by personal example. I thought of Sam Long and Scag, of Staff Sergeant Kittle—they had been examples of what a sergeant should be. If a noncommissioned officer is dedicated to his troops, the squad or section will have hard, realistic training, hot food when it's available, and the chance to take an occasional shower. If a sergeant is indifferent to the needs of his soldiers, their performance

will suffer, and their lives might be wasted. A smart officer works hard to develop good NCOs.[1]

The American military understands the value of leadership and always places a high value on it. If you value leadership, leaders will emerge to add value to the organization.

This time the question to ask yourself is very simple: Do I place a high value on leadership in my organization?

4. Look for Potential Leaders

If leadership is on your radar and you value it, you will continually be on the lookout for potential leaders. Several years ago I did a lesson for one of my leadership development tape clubs that taught leaders what to look for in potential leaders. It was called "Searching for Eagles," and for many years it was our most requested lesson. These are the top ten characteristics of "eagles":

- They make things happen.
- They see opportunities.
- They influence the opinions and actions of others.
- They add value to you.
- They draw winners to them.

- They equip other eagles to lead.
- They provide ideas that help the organization.
- They possess an uncommonly great attitude.
- They live up to their commitments.
- They show fierce loyalty to the organization and the leader.

As you begin to search for potential leaders, look for people who possess these qualities. Meanwhile, ask yourself: *Am I continually looking for potential leaders?*

5. KNOW AND RESPECT YOUR PEOPLE

As you find leaders and develop them, you will get to know them better as individuals. But there are also other characteristics that are common to all leaders that you should keep in mind as you take them through the development process.

- People want to see results.
- People want to be effective—they want to do what they do well.
- People want to be in the picture.
- People want to be appreciated.
- People want to be a part of the celebration.

As you select people to develop, work to strike a balance between these universal desires and the individual needs of your people. Try to tailor the development process for each individual as much as you can. To do that, continually ask yourself, *Do I know and respect my people?*

6. Provide Your People with Leadership Experiences

It is impossible to learn leadership without actually leading. After all, leadership is action. One of the places where many leaders miss developmental opportunities comes in what we delegate. Our natural tendency is to give others tasks to perform rather than leadership functions to fulfill. We need to make a shift. If we don't delegate leadership—with authority as well as accountability—our people will never gain the experience they need to lead well.

The question you must ask yourself is, Am I providing my people with leadership experiences?

7. Reward Leadership Initiative

Taking initiative is such an important part of leadership. The best leaders are proactive. They make things happen. Most leaders are initiators, but that doesn't mean that every leader feels comfortable when others use their initiative. Just because they trust their own instincts doesn't mean they trust the instincts of their people.

It's true that emerging leaders often want to take the lead before they are really ready to. But potential leaders can only become full-fledged leaders if they are allowed to develop and use their initiative. So what's the solution? Good timing! If you rush the timing, you short-circuit the growth process. If you hold leaders back when they're ready to move, you stunt their growth.

One of the things that can help you navigate the timing issue is recognizing whether your mind-set is one of scarcity or abundance. If you believe that the world has only a limited amount of resources, a finite number of opportunities, and so forth, then you may be reluctant to let your leaders take risks—because you may think that the organization will not be able to recover from mistakes. On the other hand, if you believe opportunities are unlimited, that resources are renewable and unlimited, you will be more willing to take risks. You will not doubt your ability to recover.

How are you doing in this area? Ask yourself, *Do I reward leadership initiative?*

8. Provide a Safe Environment Where People Ask Questions, Share Ideas, and Take Risks

Pulitzer Prize–winning historian Garry Wills said, "Leaders have a say in what they are being led to. A leader who neglects that soon finds himself without followers." It takes secure leaders at the top to let the leaders working for them be full participants in the organization's leadership process. If leaders in the middle question them, they don't take it personally. When they share ideas, the leaders cannot afford to feel threatened. When people lower than they are in the organization want to take risks, they need to be willing to give them room to succeed or fail.

Leadership by its very nature challenges. It challenges out-of-date ideas. It challenges old ways of doing things. It challenges the status quo. Never forget that what gets rewarded gets done. If you reward complacency, you will get complacency from your leaders in the middle. But if you can remain secure and let them find new ways of doing things—ways that are better than yours—the organization will move forward more quickly.

Instead of trying to be Mr. Answerman or Ms. Fix-it, when your leaders start coming into their own, move more into the background. Try taking on the role of wise counselor and chief encourager. Welcome the desire of your best leaders to innovate and improve the organization. After all, I think you'll agree that a win for the organization is a win for you.

So what role are you playing in your organization? Are you "the expert," or are you more of an advisor and advocate? Ask yourself, *Am I providing an environment where people can ask questions, share ideas, and take risks?*

9. GROW WITH YOUR PEOPLE

I've talked to a lot of leaders during my career, and I've detected a number of different attitudes toward growth. Here's how I would summarize them:

- I have already grown.
- I want my people to grow.
- I'm dedicated to helping my people grow.
- I want to grow along with my people.

Guess which attitude fosters an organization where people are growing?

When people in an organization see the leader growing, it changes the culture of the organization. It immediately removes many barriers between the leader and the rest of the people, putting you on the same level with them, which makes the leader much more human and accessible. It also sends a clear message to everyone: make growth a priority.

So the question I want you to ask yourself is very simple: *Am I growing with my people?*

10. Draw People with High Potential into Your Inner Circle

When Mark Sanborn, author of *The Fred Factor*, spoke at one of our leadership events, he made a remark that really stuck with me: "It's better to have a group of deer led by a lion than a group of lions led by a deer." Why? Because even if you have a group of deer, if they are led by a lion, they will act like a pride of lions. Isn't that a great analogy? It's really true. When people spend time with someone and are directed by them, they learn to think the way that person thinks and do what that person does. Their performance starts to rise according to the capability of their leader.

When I was working on *Developing the Leaders Around You*, I often took an informal poll at conferences to find out how people came to be leaders. I asked if they became leaders because (a) they were given a position; (b) there was a crisis in the organization; or (c) they had been mentored. More than 80 percent indicated that they were leaders because someone had mentored them in leadership—had taken them through the process.

The best way to develop high-caliber leaders is to have them mentored by a high-caliber leader. If you lead your organization, you are probably the best (or at least one of the best) leader in the organization. If you are not already doing so, you need to handpick the people with the greatest potential, invite them into your inner circle, and mentor them. It doesn't matter if you do it with one or with a dozen, whether you work one-on-one or in a group setting. The main thing is that you need to be giving your best to your best people.

Are you doing that? What is your answer to the question, Am I drawing people with potential into my inner circle?

11. COMMIT YOURSELF TO DEVELOPING A LEADERSHIP TEAM

When I started out as a leader, I tried to do everything myself. Until I was about age forty, I thought I could do it all. After my fortieth birthday, I finally realized that if I didn't develop other leaders, my potential was only a fraction of what it could be. So for the next decade, developing people into good leaders was my focus. But even that has its limitations. I realize now that to reach the highest level of leadership, I must continually develop leadership teams.

Let's face it. No one does everything well. I can't do it all—can you? I wrote the *The 21 Irrefutable Laws of Leadership*, which contains every leadership principle I know based on a lifetime of learning and leading. I can't do all of the twenty-one laws well. So I need help.

You do too. If you want your organization to reach its potential, if you want it to go from good to great (or even average to good), you need to develop a team of leaders, people who can fill in each other's gaps, people who challenge and sharpen one another. If we try to do it all ourselves, we will never get beyond the glass ceiling of our own leadership limitations.

How are you in this area? Ask yourself, Am I committed to developing a leadership team?

12. Unleash Your Leaders to Lead

As leaders, if we feel any uncertainty or insecurity about the leadership development process, it is usually not related to the training we give. The uncertainty we feel comes when we contemplate releasing our leaders to lead. It is not dissimilar to what parents feel with their kids. My children are grown and have families of their own, but when they were teenagers, the hardest thing for my wife and me was releasing them to go their own way and make their own decisions. It is scary, but if you don't let them try out their wings, they will never learn to fly.

As I have grown older, I have come to think of myself as a lid lifter. That is my main function as a team leader. If I can lift the leadership lids for the members of my team, then I am doing my job. The more barriers I remove for my people, the more likely they are to rise up to their potential. And what's really great is that when the leaders are lid lifters for the leaders in the middle of an organization, then those leaders become load lifters for the ones at the top. If you become dedicated to developing and releasing team leaders, your organization will change—and so will your life.

PART II

THE DYNAMICS OF TEAMWORK

5

WHAT ARE THE CHARACTERISTICS OF A GOOD TEAM?

Great teams have everyone on the same page.

In all my years of people development and team building, I have found that all successful teams share some common characteristics. If you, as a player, team leader, or coach, can cultivate these qualities in your group of leaders, they will become a cohesive team capable of leaping tall buildings or performing any other required task. Here are those characteristics:

THE TEAM MEMBERS CARE FOR ONE ANOTHER

All great teams begin with this quality. It is the foundation upon which everything is built. Teams that don't bond can't build. Why? Because they never become a cohesive unit.

One of the best descriptions of this quality that I've ever come across was given by college football coach Lou Holtz.

He said that he had once watched a television program that examined why men died for their country. In the program, which looked at United States Marines, the French Foreign Legion, and the British Commandos, it was noted that men died for their country because of the love they had for their fellow man. In the show, they interviewed a soldier who had been wounded in combat and was recovering in a hospital when he heard his unit was going back out on a dangerous mission. The soldier escaped from the hospital and went with them, only to be wounded again. When asked why he did it, he said that after you work and live with people, you soon realize your survival depends on one another. For a team to be successful, the teammates have to know they will look out for one another.

I have found that one of the best ways to get members of a team to care about one another is to get them together outside of a work context in order to build relationships. Every year in our organization we plan retreats and other events that put our people together in social settings. And during those times, we also make sure they spend part of their time with staff members they don't know very well. That way they're not only building relationships, they're being prevented from developing cliques.

The Team Members Know What Is Important

One of the things I enjoy most about a team experience is how the team functions as a single unit. All of its parts have a common goal and purpose. This quality is developed by making sure each team member knows what is important to the team. This quality, like the previous one, is foundational to team building. Without it team members cannot truly work together.

In a sport such as basketball, the players on a team recognize that scoring is what is important. When a team is more effective at scoring than the opponent, it wins. Because the team members know that, they spend their time improving and perfecting their ability to score. That is their focus. In contrast, in many organizational settings, the team members don't know what it means to "score." They may have a list of duties, but they don't know how those duties go together to make a score. It would be the equivalent of a basketball player who knew how to set a pick, dribble, and pass, but who never knew all these skills were used together to score baskets.

If just one player on a basketball team doesn't know what is important to the team, it makes him ineffective. And when he is in the game, it is impossible for the team to succeed. The same is true in any organization. Anyone who doesn't know what's important to the team not only fails to contribute to the team, but actually *prevents the team from achieving success.* That is why it is so important for the leader of the team to identify what is important to the team and to communicate that information to her team members.

The Team Members Communicate with One Another

The third foundational quality of an effective team is communication. Just as it is important for the team leader to communicate what is important to the team, the individual members of the team must communicate with one another. Without it, the players are likely to work against each other. Important tasks can be left undone, and team members can find themselves duplicating work.

Anyone who has played basketball is familiar with the situation in which two players go up for a rebound and fight each other for the ball, only to find that they are on the same team. On teams where players communicate with one another, a third player will shout, "Same team!" to make sure they don't lose the ball while trying to take it away from one another. That is what communication on the team is all about: letting each other know what's going on so the team's best interest is protected.

The same is true in nonsporting organizations. Clear and formal lines of communication must be established. But even more important, an atmosphere of positive communication must be established and encouraged on a daily basis. People on the team must be made to feel that they are in an environment where it is safe to offer suggestions or criticism without feeling threatened, freely trade information in the spirit of cooperation, and discuss ideas without being negatively criticized. Open communication among teammates increases productivity.

THE TEAM MEMBERS GROW TOGETHER

Once the members of the team care for one another, have a common goal, and communicate with one another, they are ready to start growing. In an organization, it is the team leader's responsibility to orchestrate the team's growth. He must make sure his people grow both personally and professionally. And he must ensure that their growth happens together—as a team.

When I work on growing my team members, I take several different approaches. First, we all learn together on a regular basis, at least once a month. In this way, I *know* there are some things everyone in the organization knows, and they share the common experience of learning these things together, regardless of their position or responsibilities.

Second, I regularly build small teams of learners. I periodically have groups of three or four work together on a project that requires them to learn. It builds strong relational bonds between those people. It's a good idea, by the way, to vary the members of these teams so that different people are learning to work together. It also gives you an idea about the particular chemistry of different groups as they work together.

Finally, I frequently send different people to conferences, workshops, and seminars. When they return, I ask them to teach others in the organization what they've learned. It gets everyone used to teaching and learning from each other. Shared experiences and the give-and-take of communication are the greatest ways to promote team growth.

THERE IS A TEAM FIT

As people who care about one another grow together and work toward a common goal, they get to know each other better. They start to appreciate each other's strengths and become aware of each other's weaknesses. They begin to recognize and appreciate each player's unique qualities. And that leads to the development of a team "fit."

The type of fit a team has depends on many things. It is more than just the way a group of people with particular talents come together. We have probably all seen teams made up of talented players at each position who should have been able to play well together but couldn't. Despite their talents, they didn't have the right chemistry.

A good team fit requires an attitude of partnership. Every team member must respect the other players. They must desire to contribute to the team, and they must come to expect a contribution from every other person. Above all, they must learn to trust each other. It is trust that makes it possible for them to rely on one another. It allows them to make up for each other's weaknesses instead of trying to exploit them. It enables one team member to say to the other, "You go ahead and do this task because you are better at it than I am," without shame or manipulation. Trust allows team members to begin working as a single unit, to begin accomplishing the things that together they recognize as important. Once the players know and trust one another, and develop a fit, the team's personality will begin to emerge.

The Team Members Place Their Individual
Rights Beneath the Best Interest of the Team

Once team members believe in the goals of their team and begin to develop genuine trust in one another, they will be in a position to demonstrate true teamwork. Their mutual trust will make it possible for them to place their own rights and privileges beneath the best interest of the team.

Notice that I mention the team members will be in a *position* to demonstrate true teamwork. That does not necessarily mean that they will. For there to be teamwork, several things must happen. First, they must genuinely believe that the value of the team's success is greater than the value of their own individual interests. They will be able to believe it only if they care about one another and if their leader has effectively cast the vision of what is important. Then they will recognize that their success will come with the team's success.

Second, for team members to place their individual rights beneath the team's best interest, personal sacrifice must be encouraged and then rewarded—by the team leader and the other members of the team. As this happens, the people will come to identify themselves more and more with the team. At that point they will recognize that individualism wins trophies, but teamwork wins pennants.

EACH TEAM MEMBER PLAYS A SPECIAL ROLE

As the team fit becomes stronger and each person is willing to put the team first, people begin to recognize their different roles on the team. They can do this because they know what must be accomplished to win, and they know their teammates' capabilities. With that knowledge and some encouragement from the team leader, people will gladly assume appropriate roles. Philip Van Auken, in *The Well-Managed Ministry*, recognizes this as the *Niche Principle*. He says, "People who occupy a special place on the team feel special and perform in a special way. Team niches humanize teamwork."

In an ideal situation, each person's role is built on his or her greatest strengths. That way each person's talents can be maximized. But it doesn't always work exactly that way. Because the team's success is what is most important, sometimes the team members must be flexible. For example, anyone who follows professional basketball has heard of Magic Johnson. He played for the Los Angeles Lakers during the 1980s, when they were one of the best teams. His greatest talent was his ability to make plays happen, especially assists using incredible look-away passes. But Johnson was a player who was always willing to fill whatever role the team needed. Over several seasons, he started in NBA championship games as a guard, forward, and center. He may be the only professional basketball player who has ever done that.

The important thing is that all the team members take a role that fits the goals and needs of the organization as well as their own personal talents and abilities. When any role is not filled, the whole team suffers.

If you are a team leader, you must recognize what roles need to be filled by your team members for the team to accomplish its goal. And when you see a role not being filled, you must make adjustments to the team to make sure the job gets done.

AN EFFECTIVE TEAM HAS A GOOD BENCH

In sports, the bench may be the most misunderstood resource of the team. Many "starting" players believe that they are important, while the people on the bench are not.

They believe they could do without them. Others who spend much of their time on the bench don't recognize their own contribution. Some mistakenly believe they don't have to bother preparing the way the starters do, that they don't have to be ready to play. But the truth is that a good bench is indispensable. Without a good bench, a team will never succeed.

The first thing a good bench gives is depth. In sports, many teams can produce a winning season. But when the level of competition goes up, such as in a play-off or a national tournament, a team without depth just can't make it. If the team does not have good reserve players, it will not be able to go the distance. I have yet to see a championship team that did not have a good bench. In fact, developing a good bench is what much of this book is about: selecting, equipping, and developing people to do their best and get the job done when they are needed.

Another property of a team's bench is that it sets the tone for the whole team's level of play. This is true because the team's preparation depends on the bench. In sports, teams practice against their own players. If the starters practice only against weak players, their performance will not improve. But a good bench causes them to do their best all the time, to constantly improve. The same is true in any organization. If the level of play in the organization is high every day, then the team's performance will be top-notch when it really counts.

Finally, a good bench is a requirement for a successful team because it provides a place for a weary player to rest. On successful teams, when one of the players cannot make it any farther due to fatigue or injury, his teammates carry the load and give him a rest. This is possibly the finest quality of teamwork—the willingness of one player to step up his level of play and go the extra mile for his teammate in a time of need. It is the ultimate indication of a player's desire to put the team and its goals first.

THE TEAM MEMBERS KNOW EXACTLY WHERE THE TEAM STANDS

In sports, the ability to know where their team stands at every moment during a game separates the great players from the adequate players. That quality, as much as talent, enables a player to move from one level of play up to the next, such as from college to the pros. Coaches have different terms for this quality. A football coach, for instance, might call it *football sense*. A basketball coach might call it *court sense* or *vision.* It is the ability to know how many seconds are left on the clock, how many points they are down, and which players are hot or hurt on each team. It is a quality that makes players, and therefore teams, great.

Outside of sports, the quality could be called *organizational sense.* It is the ability to know what is happening within the organization, how the organization stands in reference to its goals, how it stacks up against the competition, how the different players are doing, and how much more they can give in order to get the team where it needs to go. Not all team members are equally gifted with this sense. It is the job of the team leader to keep all of the players informed. He must get them to check on the team's progress and listen to the other players to know where the team stands. If all the team members are informed of where the team stands, they are in a better position to know what it is going to take for the team to succeed.

The Team Members Are Willing to Pay the Price

Time after time, success comes down to sacrifice—willingness to pay the price. The same is true of a winning team. Each member of the team must be willing to sacrifice time and energy to practice and prepare. He must be willing to be held accountable. He must be willing to sacrifice his own desires. He must be willing to give up part of himself for the team's success.

It all comes down to the desire and dedication of the individuals on the team. It's as true in business as it is in sports. It's even true in war. In an interview with David Frost, General Norman Schwarzkopf, commander of the Allied forces in the Gulf War, was asked, "What's the greatest lesson you've learned out of all this?" He replied:

> I think that there is one really fundamental military truth. And that's that you can add up the correlation of forces, you can look at the number of tanks, you can look at the number of airplanes, you can look at all these factors of military might and put them together. But unless the soldier on the ground, or the airman in the air, has the will to win, has the strength of character to go into battle, believes that his cause is just, and has the support of his country . . . all the rest of that stuff is irrelevant.

Without each person's conviction that the cause is worth the price, the battle will never be won, and the team will not succeed. There must be commitment.

When you build a team within your organization, you will be capable of a level of success you never thought possible. Teamwork for a worthwhile vision makes it possible for common people to attain uncommon results. And when the team members are not common people, but leaders, their accomplishments can multiply.

6

WHAT DOES IT MEAN
TO BE A TEAM PLAYER?

The best players put the team first.

When the situation is life or death, most people worry more about taking care of themselves than anyone else. Not Philip Toosey. As an officer in the British army during World War II, he had plenty of opportunities to preserve himself, but instead, he always looked out for his team.

In 1927, when the twenty-three-year-old Toosey joined the Territorial Army, a kind of army reserve, he did so because he wanted to do more than merely develop in his career in banking and commodities trading. He had other interests. He was a good athlete and enjoyed playing rugby, but many of his friends were applying for service, so he decided to join as well. He was commissioned as a second lieutenant in an artillery unit, where he excelled as a leader and battery commander. In time, he moved up in rank to major.

In 1939, he and his unit were called up to active service as war broke out in Europe. He briefly served in France, was evacuated at Dunkirk, and was subsequently shipped overseas to serve in the Pacific. There he was part of the failed attempt to defend the Malay Peninsula and then finally Singapore from Japanese aggression. By that time, Toosey had been promoted to lieutenant colonel and was in command of the 135th regiment of the army's Eighteenth Division. And although he and his men fought well during the campaign, British forces were repeatedly required to retreat until they fell all the way back to Singapore.

It was there that Toosey displayed the first of many characteristically unselfish acts. When the British realized that surrender was inevitable, Toosey was ordered to leave his men and ship out so that his expertise as an artillery officer might be preserved and used elsewhere. He refused. He later recalled:

> I could not really believe my ears but being a Territorial [rather than a regular army officer] I refused. I got a tremendous rocket and was told to do as I was told. However I was able to say that as a Territorial all orders were a subject of discussion. I pointed out that as a Gunner I

had read the Manual of Artillery Training, Volume II, which says quite clearly that in any withdrawal the Commanding Officer leaves last.[1]

He knew the negative effect that abandoning his men would have on their morale, so he stayed with them. Accordingly, when the Allied forces in Singapore surrendered to the Japanese in February 1942, Toosey became a prisoner of war along with his men.

Toosey soon found himself in a POW camp at Tamarkan near a major river called the Kwae Yai. As senior officer, he was in command of the Allied prisoners. His assignment from the Japanese was to build bridges across the river. (*The Bridge on the River Kwai* was based on the events that occurred at this camp, but Toosey was nothing like the character Colonel Nicholson in the movie.)

When first confronted by the orders of his Japanese captors, Toosey wanted to refuse. After all, the Hague Convention of 1907, which the Japanese had ratified, prohibited prisoners of war from being forced to do work that would help their enemies in the war effort. But Toosey also knew that refusal would bring reprisals, which he described as "immediate, physical, and severe."[2] Biographer Peter N.

Davies observed, "Toosey, in fact, quickly realized that he had no real option in this matter and accepted that the vital question was not whether the troops were to perform the tasks laid down, but how many were to die in the process."[3]

Toosey chose to ask the prisoners to cooperate with their captors, but he risked his life daily by standing up for his men and arguing for increased rations, regular working hours, and a day off each week. He later said, "If you took responsibility as I did, it increased your suffering very considerably."[4] He suffered regular beatings and was made to stand at attention in the sun for twelve hours, yet his badgering caused improved conditions for the prisoners. And remarkably, during the ten months that work was being done on the bridges, only nine prisoners died.

Later, as the commander of a POW camp hospital, Toosey was known to do everything possible to aid the welfare of his men, including hiking to meet in person every single group of prisoners who arrived at the camp, even in the dead of night. He worked with the black market in order to obtain medicine, food, and other supplies, even though detection would have meant certain death. He insisted on taking responsibility for an illegal radio if it were to be found by Japanese guards. And when the war ended, Toosey's first concern was to find the men of his regiment. He traveled three hundred miles to be reunited with them and determine that they were safe.

After he returned to England, Toosey took three weeks of vacation and then went back to his prewar work with the merchant bank Barings. He never sought glory for his endeavors during the war, nor did he complain about the movie *The Bridge on the River Kwai*, though he evidently hated it. The only thing in his later life related to the war was his work for the Far East Prisoners of War Federation to help other former POWs. It was another act characteristic of a man who always put his team ahead of himself.

CULTIVATING SELFLESSNESS

Poet W. H. Auden quipped, "We're here on earth to do good for others. What the others are here for, I don't know." No team succeeds unless its players put others on the team ahead of themselves. Being selfless isn't easy, but it is necessary.

As a team member, how do you cultivate an attitude of selflessness? Begin by doing the following:

1. Be Generous

St. Francis of Assisi stated, "All getting separates you from others; all giving unites to others." The heart of self-lessness is generosity. It not only helps to unite the team, but it also helps to advance the team. If team members are willing to give of themselves generously to the team, then it is being set up to succeed.

2. Avoid Internal Politics

One of the worst forms of selfishness can be seen in people who are playing politics on the team by posturing or positioning themselves for their own benefit, regardless of how it might damage relationships on the team. But good team players worry about the benefit of their teammates more than themselves. That kind of unselfishness helps teammates and benefits the giver. The remarkable scientist Albert Einstein observed, "A person first starts to live when he can live outside of himself."

3. Display Loyalty

If you show loyalty to the people on your team, they will return loyalty in kind. That was certainly the case for Colonel Toosey. Time and time again, he put himself on the line for his men, and as a result they worked hard, served him well, and completed whatever mission they had been given—even in the most difficult of circumstances. Loyalty fosters unity, and unity breeds team success.

4. VALUE INTERDEPENDENCE OVER INDEPENDENCE

In America, we value independence highly because it is often accompanied by innovation, hard work, and a willingness to stand for what's right. But independence taken too far is a characteristic of selfishness, especially if it begins to harm or hinder others. Seneca asserted, "No man can live happily who regards himself alone, who turns everything to his own advantage. You must live for others if you wish to live for yourself."

TO BECOME MORE SELFLESS . . .

PROMOTE SOMEONE OTHER THAN YOURSELF

If you are in the habit of talking up your achievements and promoting yourself to others, determine to keep silent about yourself and praise others for two weeks. Find positive things to say about people's actions and qualities, especially to their superiors, family, and close friends.

TAKE A SUBORDINATE ROLE

Most people's natural tendency is to take the best place and to let others fend for themselves. All day today, practice the discipline of serving, letting others go first, or taking a subordinate role. Do it for a week and see how it affects your attitude.

GIVE SECRETLY

Writer John Bunyan maintained, "You have not lived today successfully unless you've done something for someone who can never repay you." If you give to others on your team without their knowing, they cannot repay you. Try it. Get in the habit of doing it, and you may not be able to stop.

7

How Do I Go About Building a Winning Team?

A leader's investment in the team pays dividends.

Everyone knows that teamwork is a good thing; in fact, it's essential! But how does it really work? What makes a winning team? Why do some teams go straight to the top, seeing their vision become reality, while others seem to go nowhere?

Teams come in all shapes and sizes. If you're married, you and your spouse are a team. If you are employed by an organization, you and your colleagues are a team. If you volunteer your time, you and your fellow workers are a team. As Dan Devine joked, "A team is a team is a team. Shakespeare said that many times." Although the gifted playwright might not have said exactly that, the concept is nonetheless true. That's why teamwork is so important.

How to Invest in Team Building

I believe that most people recognize that investing in team building brings benefits to everyone on the team. The question for most people isn't *why*, but *how*. Allow me to share with you ten steps you can take to invest in building your team. You can implement these practices whether you are a player or coach, employee or employer, follower or leader. There is always someone on the team who can benefit from what you have to offer. And when everyone on the team is investing, then the benefits are like those of compound interest. They multiply. Here is how to get started:

1. Make the Decision to Build a Team ...
This Starts the Investment in the Team

It's said that every journey begins with the first step. Deciding that people on the team are worth developing is the first step in building a better team. That requires *commitment.*

2. Gather the Best Team Possible ...
This Elevates the Potential of the Team

As I've previously mentioned, the better the people on the team, the greater the potential. There's only one kind of team that you may be a part of where you *shouldn't* go out and find the best players available, and that's family. You need to stick with those teammates through thick and thin. But every other kind of team can benefit from the recruitment of the very best people available.

3. Pay the Price to Develop the Team . . .
This Ensures the Growth of the Team

When Morgan Wootten extended himself to benefit the kid who had two and a half strikes against him, he and his family had to pay a price to help that boy. It wasn't convenient or comfortable. It cost them in energy, money, and time.

It will cost you to develop your team. You will have to dedicate time that could be used for personal productivity. You will have to spend money that could be used for personal benefit. And sometimes you will have to set aside your personal agenda. But the benefit to the individuals—and the team—is worth the price. Everything you give is an investment.

4. Do Things Together as a Team . . .
This Provides Community for the Team

I once read the statement, "Even when you've played the game of your life, it's the feeling of teamwork that you'll remember. You'll forget the plays, the shots, and the scores, but you'll never forget your teammates." That describes the community that develops among teammates who spend time doing things together.

The only way to develop community and cohesiveness among your teammates is to get them together, not just in a professional setting but in personal ones as well. There are lots of ways to get yourself connected with your teammates, and to connect them with one another. Many families who want to bond find that camping does the trick. Business colleagues can socialize outside of work (in an appropriate way). The *where* and *when* are not as important as the fact that team members share common experiences.

5. EMPOWER TEAM MEMBERS WITH RESPONSIBILITY AND AUTHORITY . . . THIS RAISES UP LEADERS FOR THE TEAM

The greatest growth for people often occurs as a result of the trial and error of personal experience. Any team that wants people to step up to a higher level of performance— and to higher levels of leadership—must give team members authority as well as responsibility. If you are a leader on your team, don't protect your position or hoard your power. Give it away. That's the only way to empower your team.

6. Give Credit for Success to the Team . . .
This Lifts the Morale of the Team

Mark Twain said, "I can live for two months on one good compliment." That's the way most people feel. They are willing to work hard if they receive recognition for their efforts. That's why Napoleon Bonaparte observed, "A soldier will fight long and hard for a bit of colored ribbon." Compliment your teammates. Talk up their accomplishments. And if you're the leader, take the blame but never the credit. Do that and your team will always fight for you.

7. Watch to See That the Investment in the
Team Is Paying Off . . . This Brings
Accountability to the Team

If you put money into an investment, you expect a return—maybe not right away, but certainly over time. How will you know whether you are gaining or losing ground on that investment? You have to pay attention to it and measure its progress.

The same is true of an investment in people. You need to observe whether you are getting a return for the time, energy, and resources you are putting into them. Some people develop quickly. Others are slower to respond, and that's okay. The main outcome you want to see is progress.

8. Stop Your Investment in Players Who Do Not Grow . . . This Eliminates Greater Losses for the Team

One of the most difficult experiences for any team member is leaving a teammate behind. Yet that is what you must do if someone on your team refuses to grow or change for the benefit of teammates. That doesn't mean that you love the person less. It just means you stop spending your time trying to invest in someone who won't or can't make the team better.

9. Create New Opportunities for the Team . . . This Allows the Team to Stretch

There is no greater investment you can make in building a team than giving it new opportunities. When a team has the possibility of taking new ground or facing new challenges, it has to stretch to meet them. That process not only gives the team a chance to grow, but it also benefits every individual. Everyone has the opportunity to grow toward his or her potential.

10. Give the Team the Best Possible Chance to Succeed . . . This Guarantees the Team a High Return

James E. Hunton says, "Coming together is a beginning. Keeping together is progress. Working together is success." One of the most essential tasks you can undertake is to clear obstacles so that the team has the best possible chance to work toward success. If you are a team member, that may mean making a personal sacrifice or helping others work together better. If you are a leader, that means creating an energized environment for the team and giving each person what he needs at any given time to ensure success.

Investing in building a team almost guarantees a high return for the effort because a team can do so much more than individuals. Or as Rex Murphy, one of my conference attendees, told me, "Where there's a will there's a way; where there's a team, there's more than one way."

HOW DOES A WEAK PLAYER
IMPACT THE TEAM?

*A weak link harms the leader's credibility
and the team's chances for success.*

As much as any team likes to measure itself by its best people, the truth is that *the strength of the team is impacted by its weakest link*. No matter how much people try to rationalize it, compensate for it, or hide it, a weak link will eventually come to light.

YOUR TEAM IS NOT FOR EVERYONE

One of the mistakes I often made early in my career as a team leader was that I thought everyone who was on my team should remain on the team. That was true for several reasons. First, I naturally see the best in people. When I look at individuals with potential, I see all that they can become—even if they don't see it. And I try to encourage and equip them to become better. Second, I truly like people. I figure the more who take the trip, the bigger the party. Third, because I have vision and believe my goals are worthwhile and beneficial, I sometimes naively assume that everyone will want to go along with me.

But just because I wanted to take everyone with me didn't mean that it would always work out that way. My first memorable experience with this occurred in 1980 when I was offered an executive position at Wesleyan World Headquarters in Marion, Indiana. When I accepted the position, I invited my assistant to come with me to be a part of the new team I was building. So she and her husband considered my offer and went to Marion to look around. I'll never forget when they came back. As I excitedly talked about the coming challenges and how we could begin to tackle them, I began to realize from the expressions on their faces that something was wrong. And that's when they told me. They weren't going.

That statement took me completely by surprise. In fact, I was sure that they were making a mistake and told them so, doing my best to convince them to change their minds. But my wife, Margaret, gave me some very good advice. She said, "John, your problem is that you want to take everybody with you. But not everyone is going to go on the journey. Let it go." It was a hard lesson for me to learn—and sometimes it still is.

From that experience and others I've had since then, I've discovered that when it comes to teamwork . . .

1. Not Everyone Will Take the Journey

Some people don't want to go. My assistant and her husband wanted to stay in Lancaster, Ohio, where they had built relationships for many years. For other people the issue is their attitude. They don't want to change, grow, or conquer new territory. They hold fast to the status quo. All you can do with people in this group is kindly thank them for their past contributions and move on.

2. Not Everyone Should Take the Journey

Other people shouldn't join a team because it's a matter of their agenda. They have other plans, and where you're going isn't the right place for them. The best thing you can do for people in this category is wish them well, and as far as you are able, help them on their way so that they achieve success in their venture.

3. NOT EVERYONE CAN TAKE THE JOURNEY

For the third group of people, the issue is ability. They may not be capable of keeping pace with their teammates or helping the group get where it wants to go. How do you recognize people who fall into this category? They're not very hard to identify.

- They can't keep pace with other team members.
- They don't grow in their area of responsibility.
- They don't see the big picture.
- They won't work on personal weaknesses.
- They won't work with the rest of the team.
- They can't fulfill expectations for their area.

If you have people who display one or more of those characteristics, then you need to acknowledge that they are weak links.

That's not to say that they are necessarily bad people. In fact, some teams exist to serve weak links or help them become stronger. It depends on the team's goals. For example, when I was a senior pastor, we reached out to people in the community with food and assistance. We helped people with addictions, divorce recovery, and many other difficulties. Our goal was to serve them. It's good and appropriate to help people who find themselves in those circumstances. But putting them on the team while they are still broken and weak doesn't help them, and it hurts the team—even to the extent of making the team incapable of accomplishing its goal of service.

What can you do with people on your team who are weak links? You really have only two choices: you need to train them or trade them. Of course, your first priority should always be to try to train people who are having a hard time keeping up. Help can come in many forms: giving people books to read, sending them to conferences, presenting them with new challenges, pairing them with mentors. I believe that people often rise to your level of expectations. Give them hope and training, and they usually improve.

But what should you do if a team member continually fails to meet expectations, even after receiving training, encouragement, and opportunities to grow? My father used to have a saying: "Water seeks its own level." Somebody who is a weak link on your team might be capable of becoming a star on another team. You need to give that person an opportunity to find his level somewhere else.

THE IMPACT OF A WEAK LINK

If you are a team leader, you cannot avoid dealing with weak links. Team members who don't carry their own weight slow down the team, and they have a negative effect on your leadership. Several things may happen when a weak link remains on the team:

1. THE STRONGER MEMBERS IDENTIFY THE WEAK ONE

A weak link cannot hide (except in a group of weak people). If you have strong people on your team, they always know who isn't performing up to the level of everyone else.

2. THE STRONGER MEMBERS HAVE TO HELP THE WEAK ONE

If your people must work together as a team to do their work, then they have only two choices when it comes to a weak teammate. They can ignore the person and allow the team to suffer, or they can help him and make the team more successful. If they are team players, they will help.

3. The Stronger Members Come to Resent the Weak One

Whether strong team members help or not, the result will always be the same: resentment. No one likes to lose or fall behind consistently because of the same person.

4. The Stronger Members Become Less Effective

Carrying someone else's load in addition to your own compromises your performance. Do that for a long time, and the whole team suffers.

5. The Stronger Members Question the Leader's Ability

Anytime the leader allows a weak link to remain a part of the team, the team members forced to compensate for the weak person begin to doubt the leader's courage and discernment. You lose the respect of the best when you don't deal properly with the worst.

Many team members may be able to avoid the hard decision of dealing with subpar members, but leaders can't. In fact, one of the differences between leaders and followers is action. Followers often know what to do, but they are unwilling or unable to follow through. But know this: if other people on the team make decisions for you because you are unwilling or unable to make them, then your leadership is being compromised, and you're not serving the team well.

Strengthening the Chain

Weak team members always take more of the team's time than strong ones. One reason is that the more competent people have to give their time to compensate for those who don't carry their share of the load. The greater the difference in competence between the more accomplished performers and the less accomplished ones, the greater the detriment to the team. For example, if you rate people on a scale from 1 to 10 (with 10 being the best), a 5 among 10s really hurts the team, where an 8 among 10s often does not.

Let me show you how this works. When you first put together a group of people, their talents come together in a way that is analogous to addition. So visually a 5 among 10s looks like this:

$$10 + 10 + 10 + 10 + 5 = 45$$

The difference between this team and great ones with five 10s is like the difference between 50 and 45. That's a difference of 10 percent. But once a team comes together and starts to develop chemistry, synergy, and momentum, it's analogous to multiplication. That's when a weak link really starts to hurt the team. It's the difference between this:

$$10 \times 10 \times 10 \times 10 \times 10 = 100,000$$

and this:

$$10 \times 10 \times 10 \times 10 \times 5 = 50,000$$

That's a difference of 50 percent! The power and momentum of the team may be able to compensate for a weak link for a while, but not forever. A weak link eventually robs the team of momentum—and potential.

Ironically, weak links are less aware than stronger members of their weaknesses and shortcomings. They also spend more time guarding their turf, saving their positions, and holding on to what they have. And know this: when it comes to interaction between people, the weaker person usually controls the relationship. For example, someone with a good self-image is more flexible than a person with a poor self-image. An individual with a clear vision acts more readily than someone without one. A person with superb ability and high energy accomplishes more and works longer than an individual with lesser gifts. If the two people journey together, the stronger member must constantly work with and wait on the weaker one. That controls what happens on the journey.

If your team has a weak link who can't or won't rise to the level of the team—and you've done everything you can to help the person improve—then you've got to take action. When you do, heed the advice of authors Danny Cox and John Hoover. If you need to remove somebody from the team, be discreet, be clear, be honest, and be brief. Then, once the person is gone, be open about it with the rest of the team while maintaining respect for the person you let go.[1] And if you start to have second thoughts before or afterward, remember this: as long as a weak link is part of the team, everyone else on the team will suffer.

9

———

How Do I Create Positive
Energy on the Team?

Put completing teammates ahead of
competing with them.

Chris Hodges, a good leader who is a native of Baton
Rouge, is well-known for telling Boudreaux jokes, a
type of humor popular in Louisiana. Recently on a trip for
EQUIP, he told me this one (I'll try to capture the accent in
writing as best I can—just think Justin Wilson):

A group of Cajuns was sitting around bragging about
how successful they were. Thibideaux says, "I just bought
me another shrimp boat, yeah, and I got me a crew of
ten people workin' for me."

"Dat ain't nottin'," says Landry. "I been promoted
at the refinery, and now I got fifty men workin' for
me."

Boudreaux hears this, and he doesn't want to look bad in front of his friends, so he says, "Oh yeah, well I got three hundred people under me."

Thibideaux says, "What you talkin' 'bout, Boudreaux? You mow lawns all day."

"Dat's true," says Boudreaux, "but now I'm cuttin' da grass at the cemetery, and I got three hundred people under me."

There's nothing wrong with competition. The problem for many leaders is that they end up competing against their peers in their own organization in a way that hurts the team and them. It all depends on how you handle competition and how you channel it. In healthy working environments, there is both competition and teamwork. The issue is to know when each is appropriate. When it comes to your teammates, you want to compete in such a way that instead of *competing* with them, you are *completing* them. Those are two totally different mind-sets.

COMPETING   VS.   COMPLETING

Competing   Completing
Scarcity mind-set   Abundance mind-set

Me first	Organization first
Destroys trust	Develops trust
Thinks win-lose	Thinks win-win
Single thinking	Shared thinking
(my good ideas)	(our great ideas)
Excluding others	Including others

Winning at all costs will cost you when it comes to your peers. If your goal is to beat your peers, then you will never be able to influence them.

How to Balance Competing and Completing

The bottom line is that the success of the whole team is more important than any individual wins. Organizations need both competition and teamwork to win. When those two elements exist in the right balance, great team chemistry is the result.

So how do you balance competing and completing? How do you learn to easily shift from one to the other? Here's what I recommend.

1. ACKNOWLEDGE YOUR NATURAL DESIRE TO COMPETE

About four or five years after I graduated from college, I went back to play in an alumni basketball game against the college's then-current team. Back when I played for the team, I had been a shooting guard, but this time they assigned me to cover the team's point guard. As I watched him in warm-ups, I knew I was in trouble. He was a lot faster than I was. So I quickly developed a strategy.

The first time he tried to take the ball inside to the hoop, I fouled him. I don't mean I tapped his hand as he shot the ball. I mean I really fouled him—hard. He got up, limped to the line for his free throws, and clanged both of them off the back of the rim. So far, so good.

The next time his team came down the floor and he tried to set up a shot from outside, I fouled him hard again. As he got up, he started grumbling under his breath.

Soon after that when there was a loose ball, I dove after it, but I also made sure I landed right on top of him. I wasn't as big then as I am now, but I was heavier than he was.

He popped up and barked at me, "You're playing too hard. It's only a game."

"Okay," I said with a grin, "then let me win."

It doesn't matter who you are or what you do, competitiveness is a natural leadership instinct. I haven't met a leader yet who didn't like to win. I look back now and recognize that I wasn't very mature. The good news is that the alumni team won the game. The bad news is that I didn't make a friend that day.

The key to being competitive is channeling it in a positive way. If you squash it, you lose an edge that motivates you to do some of your best work. If you let it run wild, you run over your teammates and alienate them. But if you control it and direct it, competitiveness can help you succeed.

2. Embrace Healthy Competition

Every winning team I've ever seen or been a part of experienced healthy competition among team members. Healthy competition does so many positive things for a team, many of which cannot be achieved through anything else.

Healthy competition helps bring out your best. How many world records do you suppose are set when a runner runs alone? I don't know of one! People function at peak capacity when they have someone else pushing them. That's true whether you're learning, practicing, or playing in the game.

Healthy competition promotes honest assessment. What is the quickest way for you to measure your effectiveness in your profession? Maybe you have long-term measurements in place, such as monthly or yearly goals. But what if you want to know how you're doing today? How would you go about measuring it? You could look at your to-do list. But what if you set the bar too low for yourself? You could ask your boss. But maybe the best way would be to see what others in your line of work are doing. If you are significantly behind or ahead of them, wouldn't that tell you something? And if you were behind, wouldn't you try to figure out what you're doing wrong? It may not be the only way to assess yourself, but it certainly can provide a good reality check.

Healthy competition creates camaraderie. When people compete together, it often creates a connection between them, whether they are on the same team or opposing teams. When competition is ongoing and friendly on the same team, it creates an even stronger bond that can lead to great camaraderie.

Healthy competition doesn't become personal. Competition between teammates is ultimately about having fun. When competition is healthy, teammates remain friends when the game is done. They play against each other for the thrill of it, and when they're done, they can walk away together without hard feelings.

I love the joke about the rooster who dragged an ostrich egg into the henhouse. He laid it down for all the hens to see and said, "I don't want to intimidate you girls, but I just want to show you what they're doing up the road." Competition can definitely help motivate a team to get going.

3. Put Competition in Its Proper Place

The whole goal of healthy competition is to leverage it for the corporate win. Competition in practice helps teammates improve one another for game day. If it is channeled correctly, it is used to beat the other team.

Of course, some leaders can take this to the extreme. Tommy Lasorda, former manager of the Los Angeles Dodgers, has told the story about the day his team was scheduled to play on the road against the Cincinnati Reds. In the morning, Lasorda went to mass. As he settled into his pew, the manager of the Reds, Johnny McNamara, happened to come into the same church and sit down in the same pew.

The men eyed one another, but neither spoke.

When mass was over, they had begun to walk out when Lasorda discovered that the other manager had paused to light a candle. He figured that gave the Reds an edge. "When he left, I went down and blew that candle out," Lasorda said. "All throughout the game, I kept hollering to him, 'Hey, Mac, it ain't gonna work. I blew it out.' We clobbered them that day, 13–2."

4. Know Where to Draw the Line

No matter how much you desire to win, if you want to cultivate the ability to compete in a healthy way, you must make sure you never cross the line by "going for the throat" with your peers, because if you do, you will alienate them. And that line is not difficult to define. I'd say that when competitiveness raises the bar and makes others better, that's healthy. Anytime it lowers morale and hurts the team, it's unhealthy and out of line.

When I was leading Skyline Church in the San Diego area, my staff was very competent and very competitive. The core group who always led the charge consisted of Dan Reiland, Sheryl Fleisher, and Tim Elmore. They all had their own departments and areas of expertise, but they were always competing, always trying to one-up each other. Their friendly competition kept them on their toes, and it inspired the rest of the staff to join in and do their best. But as hard-driving and competitive as they were, if any one of them had a problem, the others were right there, ready to jump in and lend a hand. They always put the team's win ahead of their own.

Today those three leaders are out doing different things in different organizations across the country, but they remain friends. They keep in touch, share stories, and still help one another whenever they can. The kind of bond that develops when you compete together doesn't die easily. They have a deep respect for each other that continues to give them credibility—and influence—with one another.

10

How Can I Harness the
Team's Creativity?

Make sure the best idea always wins.

Imagine that you're getting ready to go into an important
project meeting that will be attended by your boss and
several people who are on the same level as you in the organization. Let's say that you were picked from among your
peers by your boss to lead the meeting, and you see this time
as your chance to shine. You've done your homework and
then some. You've spent countless hours thinking through
the project, brainstorming, planning, and endeavoring to
foresee any obstacles that could be ahead. Based on your
preliminary discussions with your staff and your peers, you
feel that your ideas are better than anything you've heard
from anyone else.

So you begin the meeting with great confidence. But
before long, the agenda is not proceeding the way you

expected or planned. Your boss makes a comment and sends the flow of the discussion in an entirely new direction. At first you think, *That's okay. I can salvage this. My ideas will still work; I just need to steer everyone back around to them.*

And then one of your peers launches in with an idea. You don't think much of it, but everyone else seems to think it's wonderful. A couple of other people in the room springboard off of that initial idea and begin to build on it. You can feel the energy in the room starting to build. Ideas are sparking. And everyone is clearly moving away from everything you've spent weeks planning—the idea that was your "baby."

What do you do?

For most people in those circumstances, their natural instinct would be to fight for their ideas. After all, by then they would have made quite an investment in them:

- *The Intellectual Investment*—it takes hours of thinking, planning, and problem solving spent to gather, create, and refine an idea.
- *The Physical Investment*—getting ready for an important meeting or presentation usually takes a lot of time, effort, and resources.

- *The Emotional Investment*—when people come up with something they see as a good idea, it's hard to keep themselves from thinking about not only what the idea could do for the company but also what it could do for them and their careers.

By this time, they become pretty attached to their ideas, and it becomes difficult to let those ideas die, especially when someone else who didn't do any work may come in and get all the credit.

Ideas: The Lifeblood of an Organization

If you desire to harness the creativity of your team, then you need to resist the temptation to fight for your idea when it's not the best idea. Why? Because good ideas are too important to the organization. Harvey Firestone, founder of the Firestone Tire and Rubber Company, said, "Capital isn't so important in business. Experience isn't so important. You can get both of these. What is important is ideas. If you have ideas, you have the main asset you need, and there isn't any limit to what you can do with your business and your life. They are any man's greatest asset—ideas."

Great organizations possess people throughout the organization who produce great ideas. That is how they become great. The progress they make and the innovations they create don't come down from on high. Their creative sessions are not dominated by top-down leaders. Nor does every meeting become a kind of wrestling match to see who can dominate everyone else. People come together as teams, peers work together, and they make progress because they want the best idea to win.

Leaders in the organization who help to surface good ideas are creating what an organization needs most. They do that by producing synergy among their peers. And they will develop influence with their peers because when they are present, they make the whole team better.

WHAT LEADS TO THE BEST IDEAS?

To let the best idea win, you must first generate good ideas. And then you must work to make them even better. How do team leaders do that? How do they help the team find the best ideas? I believe they follow this pattern:

1. Team Leaders Listen to All Ideas

Finding good ideas begins with an open-minded willingness to listen to all ideas. Mathematician and philosopher Alfred North Whitehead said, "Almost all really new ideas have a certain aspect of foolishness when they are first produced." During the brainstorming process, shutting down any ideas might prevent you from discovering the good ones.

In *Thinking for a Change*, one of the eleven thinking skills I recommend people learn is shared thinking. It is faster than solo thinking, is more innovative, and has greater value. Most important, I believe, is the fact that great thinking comes when good thoughts are shared in a collaborative environment where people contribute to them, shape them, and take them to the next level. A good team leader helps to create such an environment.

2. Team Leaders Never Settle for Just One Idea

I think many times leaders are too quick to settle on one idea and run with it. That is because leaders are so action oriented. They want to go. They want to make something happen. They want to take the hill! The problem is that they sometimes fight their way to the top of the hill only to find that it's not the right one.

One idea is never enough. Many ideas make us stronger. I once heard an analyst say he thought that was the reason the communist bloc fell at the end of the twentieth century. Communism created a system based primarily on only one idea. If anyone tried to do things a different way, they were knocked down or shipped out.

In contrast, democracy is a system based on a multitude of ideas. If people want to try something different, they have the chance to float their idea and see what happens. If it catches on, it moves forward. If not, it is replaced by another idea. Because of that freedom, in democratic countries creativity is high, opportunities are unlimited, and the potential for growth is astounding. The democratic system can be messy, but that is also true of any endeavor that's creative and collaborative.

The same kind of free-market mentality that drives the largest economy in the world can also drive organizations. If people are open to ideas and options, they can keep growing, innovating, and improving.

3. TEAM LEADERS LOOK IN UNUSUAL PLACES FOR IDEAS

Good leaders are attentive to ideas; they are always searching for them. And they cultivate that attentiveness and practice it as a regular discipline. As they read the newspaper, watch a movie, listen to their colleagues, or enjoy a leisure activity, they are always on the lookout for ideas or practices they can use to improve their work and their leadership.

If you desire to find good ideas, you have to search for them. Rarely does a good idea come looking for you.

4. Team Leaders Don't Let Personality Overshadow Purpose

When someone you don't like or respect suggests something, what is your first reaction? I bet it's to dismiss it. You've heard the phrase "Consider the source." That's not a bad thing to do, but if you're not careful, you may very likely throw out the good with the bad.

Don't let the personality of someone you work with cause you to lose sight of the greater purpose, which is to add value to the team and advance the organization. If that means listening to the ideas of people with whom you have no chemistry, or worse, a difficult history, so be it. Set aside your pride and listen. And in cases where you must reject the ideas of others, make sure you reject only the idea and not the person.

5. TEAM LEADERS PROTECT CREATIVE PEOPLE AND THEIR IDEAS

Ideas are such fragile things, especially when they first come to light. Advertising executive Charlie Brower said, "A new idea is delicate. It can be killed by a sneer or a yawn; it can be stabbed to death by a quip and worried to death by a frown on the right man's brow."

If you desire the best idea to win, then become a champion of creative people and their contributions to your organization. When you discover peers who are creative, promote them, encourage them, and protect them. Pragmatic people often shoot down the ideas of creative people. Leaders who value creativity can help the creative people around them thrive and keep generating ideas that benefit the organization.

6. TEAM LEADERS DON'T TAKE REJECTION PERSONALLY

When your ideas are not received well by others, do your best not to take it personally. When someone in a meeting does that, it can kill the creative process, because at that point the discussion is no longer about the ideas or helping the organization; it becomes about the person whose feelings are hurt. In those moments, if you can stop competing and focus your energy on creating, you will open the way for the people around you to take their creativity to the next level.

Mel Newhoff is executive vice president of Bozell Worldwide, a top advertising agency. In his industry, ideas are everything. Newhoff has some good advice about the big picture concerning ideas and how to approach your interaction with others in relation to them:

Be passionate about your work, and have the integrity to stand up for your ideas. But also know when to compromise.

Without passion you will not be taken seriously. If you don't defend your ideas, no one else will either. When principle is involved, don't budge.

But there is another side to this also. There are very few real "absolutes" in life. Most matters involve taste or opinion, not principle. In these areas recognize that you can compromise. If you become someone who can never compromise, you will forfeit opportunities to those who can.

Being an encouraging leader and leading across is not about getting your own way. It's not about winning at all costs. It's about winning respect and influence with your peers so that you can help the whole team win. Should you be passionate and determined, believing in yourself and your ability to contribute? Definitely. Should you hold on to your deeply held values and stand on principle when those are in jeopardy? Absolutely. But never forget that having a collaborative spirit helps the organization. When you think in terms of *our* idea instead of *my* idea or *her* idea, you're probably on track to helping the team win. That should be your motivation, not just trying to win friends and influence people. But I think you'll find that if you let the best idea win, you will win friends and influence people.

NOTES

CHAPTER 2

1. Lt. Commander Smith's description was so complex and detailed that I asked him to e-mail it to me so that I could describe it accurately in this book.

2. Michael Jordan and Mark Vancil, *I Can't Accept Not Trying* (San Francisco: Harper, 1994).

CHAPTER 3

1. "Mount Everest History/Facts," www.mnteverst.com.

2. James Ramsey Ullman, *Man of Everest: The Autobiography of Tenzing* (London: George G. Harrap and Co., 1955), 250.

3. Ibid., 255.

CHAPTER 4

1. Tommy Franks and Malcolm McConnell, *American Soldier* (New York: Regan Books, 2004), 99.

CHAPTER 6

1. Peter N. Davies, *The Man Behind the Bridge: Colonel Toosey and the River Kwai* (London: Athlone Press, 1991), 56.

2. Ibid., 107–8.

3. Ibid., 99.

4. "A Tale of Two Rivers," *Electronic Recorder*, March 1998, www. livgrad.co.uk.

CHAPTER 8

1. Danny Cox with John Hoover, *Leadership When the Heat's On* (New York: McGraw-Hill, 1992), 69–70.

ABOUT THE AUTHOR

JOHN C. MAXWELL is an internationally recognized leadership expert, speaker, and author who has sold over 16 million books. EQUIP, which he founded in 1996, has trained more than 2 million leaders worldwide. Every year he speaks to Fortune 500 companies, international government leaders, and audiences as diverse as the United States Military Academy at West Point, the National Football League, and ambassadors at the United Nations.

0823